A Lyric Hammersmith Production in association with Belvoir, Sydney

SEVENTEEN

By Matthew Whittet

**This play was first performed at Belvoir, Sydney
on 01 August 2015.**

**First performance of this production at the Lyric Hammersmith
on 04 Mar 2017.**

#Seventeen

Facebook: /Lyric Hammersmith
Twitter: @LyricHammer
Instagram /lyrichammersmith

SEVENTEEN

By Matthew Whittet

Cast in alphabetical order

Lizzie **Sarah Ball**
Mike **Michael Feast**
Ronnie **Mike Grady**
Jess **Diana Hardcastle**
Emilia **Margot Leicester**
Tom **Roger Sloman**

Creative Team

Directed by **Anne-Louise Sarks**
Design by **Tom Scutt**
Lighting by **Paule Constable**
Sound by **Nick Manning**
Movement Director **Imogen Knight**

Company Stage Manager **Claire Bryan**
Deputy Stage Manager **Helen King**
Assistant Stage Manager **Lucy Holland**

Casting Advisor **Amy Ball**
Assistant Director **Paloma Oakenfold**
Vocal Work by **James Fortune**
Associate Designer **Rosie Elnile**
Physiotherapist **Ava Katics**

Senior Producer **Imogen Kinchin**
Producer **Peter Holland**
Assistant Producer **Sarah Georgeson**
Production Manager **Seamus Benson**
Set Construction **Scott Fleary Productions Ltd**
Lighting Equipment supplied by **White Light Ltd**
Costume Supervisor **Ellen McQuaid**
Dresser **Harry Whitham**

Press Agency **Jo Allan PR**
Marketing Photography **Jay Brooks**

With thanks to Brenna Hobson, TEAfilms, Anthea Williams, Peter Carroll, Maggie Dence, John Gaden, Genevieve Lemon, Barry Otto, Anna Volska, Fran Rafferty, Madeline Charlemagne, Adrian Marcelo, Joseph Vaiana, Ben Butler, Nadine Elghool, Billie Morrison, Thomas Ryan, Paul Jackson, Mel Page, Bob Cousins, Nate Edmondson, Alan John, Luke McGettigan, Sara Black, Scott Witt, Vanessa Martin.

Thank you to the Circle of Seventeen for supporting this production.

Special thanks to Richard Cordery, Simon Stephens, Stanley Heath Stephens and Scarlett Heath Stephens.

MATTHEW WHITTET (Writer)

Matthew is a playwright and actor. He graduated from NIDA's acting course and was a 2013/2014 Sidney Myer Creative Fellow.

Writing credits include: *Cinderella, Old Man* (Belvoir); *Girl Asleep, Fugitive, School Dance, Big Bad Wolf* (Windmill Theatre); *Harbinger* (Brink Productions) and *Silver* (B Sharp) – Winner 2010 Philip Parsons Young Playwright's Award and *Girl Asleep* (2015 Adelaide Film Festival).

Theatre credits include: *silver* (B Sharp); *Cinderella, Conversation Piece, The Book of Everything, The Threepenny Opera, The Underpants, King Ubu, As You Like It* (Belvoir); *The Wonderful World of Dissocia, Metamorphosis, Endgame, Fireface* (Sydney Theatre Company); *Hamlet, King Lear* (Bell Shakespeare); *Moving Target, The Ham Funeral* (Malthouse) and *The Department* (State Theatre Company of South Australia).

Film and television credits include: *The Great Gatsby, Sleeping Beauty, Australia, Moulin Rouge!* and *Girl Asleep.*

CAST

SARAH BALL Lizzy
For the Lyric: *After Mrs Rochester*
Other theatre credits include: *Sheppey* (Orange Tree); *Superior Donuts* (Southwark Playhouse); *The Revengers Tragedy* (Hoxton Hall); *The Real Thing* (West Yorkshire Playhouse/ETT); *The Riots* (Tricycle); *A Doll's House, Getting Married* (Manchester Library); *Death of a Salesman* (West Yorkshire Playhouse); *Lifex3* (Watermill); *Eve and Eva* (Soho); *Absent Friends* (Salisbury Playhouse); *Jane Eyre* (Shared Experience Tour/West End); *All The Ordinary Angels, The Baby and Fly Pie* (Manchester Royal Exchange); *Antony and Cleopatra, Much Ado About Nothing, King Lear, The Tempest* and *Bingo* (RSC); *The Erpingham Camp* (Liverpool Everyman/Assembly Rooms); *Private Lives, A Doll's House, The Good Doctor* (Century); *Richard III* (Derby Playhouse); *The Killing Floor* (Bridewell) and *Mad Forest* (Royal Court).
Film and television credits include: *Moving On, Guilt, Father Brown, Lucky Man, Spotless, Doctors, Skins, Da Vinci's Demons, Holby City, The Riots: In their Own Words, Outnumbered, Marchlands, Breaking the Mould, The Bill, A Touch of Frost, Casualty, Hunter, Murphy's Law, The Fixer, Torn, Wire in the Blood, Tchaikovsky, Abolition, Life Begins, Midsomer Murders, Drive, In Deep, This Way Out, The Living and the Dead* and *The Feast of the Goat.*

MICHAEL FEAST Mike
For the Lyric: *saved, The Servant, Oliver Twist*
Other theatre credits include: *Murder in the Cathedral, Measure for Measure, Faust* (RSC); *Ross, A Month in the Country, Twelfth Night, The Master and Margarita, The Seagull, A Christmas Carol, Vivat! Vivat Regina!, Doctor Faustus, Nathan the Wise* (Chichester Festival Theatre); *The Resistible Rise of Arturo Ui* (Duchess); *Macbeth* (Gielgud/Lyceum, Broadway); *The Caretaker* (Gate, Dublin); *Ghost From a Perfect Place* (Arcola); *Facts* (Finborough); *Three Sisters* (Young Vic); *Hair* – original cast (Shaftesbury); *Pygmalion* (Garrick); *The Accused* (Haymarket); *Phaedra* (Donmar Warehouse); *The Ones That Flutter* (Theatre503); *The King's Speech* (Wyndham's); *The Forest, The Tempest, Watch It Come Down* (National Theatre); *The World's Biggest Diamond, The Shawl, Prairie du Chien, Ourselves Alone* (Royal Court) and *No Man's Land* (National Theatre/Wyndham's).
Film and television credits include: *game of Thrones, State of Play, The Steven Lawrence Case, Fantastic Fear of Everything, The Deaths of Ian Stone, Penelope, Long Time Dead, Young Blades, Sleepy Hollow, Prometheus, The Fool, Brother Sun Sister Moon, The Draughtsman's Contract* and *Velvet Goldmine.*

MIKE GRADY Ronny

Theatre credits include: *taken At Midnight* (Theatre Royal Haymarket/Chichester Festival Theatre); *Black Comedy* (Chichester Festival Theatre); *Henry VI* (Shakespeare's Globe); *Much Ado About Nothing* (Wyndham's); *Measure For Measure* (Complicité/National Theatre); *His Girl Friday* (National Theatre); *Flamingos* (Bush); *Hamlet* (Stratford East) and *Aladdin* (Everyman Cheltenham).

Film and television credits include: *Last of the Summer Wine, The Dumping Ground, Holby City, Skins, Citizen Smith, Doctors, An Ungentlemanly Act, Up The Garden Path, Sweet Sixteen, Not With A Bang, Colin's Sandwich, Chish 'N' Fips, Sherlock Holmes 2, The Return Of The Pink Panther, Bert Rigby You're A Fool, The Prisoner Of Zenda, Britannia Hospital, The Pirates Of Penzance* and *Carry On Loving*.

DIANA HARDCASTLE Jess

For the Lyric: *The London Cuckolds*.

Other theatre credits include: *the Argument* (Hampstead); *A Delicate Balance, Camera Obscura* (Almeida); *Les Liaisons Dangereuses, Ion, New England, A Patriot for Me, The Winter's Tale, A Doll's House* (RSC); *An English Tragedy, Me and Mamie O'Rourke, The Glass Menagerie* (Watford Palace); *The Vortex, The Duchess of Malfi, A Woman of No Importance* (Royal Exchange); *Tejas Verdes, A Kind of Alaska, A Slight Ache* (Gate); *Simpatico* (Royal Court); *In Remembrance of Things Past, Mutabilitie, The School for Scandal* and *The Secret Rapture* (National Theatre).

Film and television credits include: *The Kennedys, The Kennedys: After Camelot, Utopia, DCI Banks, Doctors, Holby City, Silent Witness, The Inspector Lynley Mysteries, Rosemary and Thyme, Midsomer Murders, Fortunes of War, Love Song, This House, That's Love, Taggart, Reilly Aces of Spies, The Boy, Jenny's Wedding, A Good Woman, The Best Exotic Marigold Hotel* and *The Second Best Exotic Marigold Hotel*.

MARGOT LEICESTER Emilia

Theatre credits include: *Charles III* (Almeida/Wyndham's/Music Box Theatre, New York); *The Knot of the Heart* (Almeida); *Broken Glass* – Best Actress, Olivier Award Nominee (National Theatre); *The Winter's Tale, To Kill a Mockingbird, Long Day's Journey Into Night, An Inspector Calls, The Glass Menagerie, Who's Afraid of Virginia Woolf* – Best Actress Manchester Theatre Awards Winner, *The Enemies Within* (Bolton Octagon); *The Sacred Flame* (ETT); *Measure For Measure, The Crucible, Macbeth* (Young Vic); *A Conversation* (Royal Exchange Manchester); *Colder Than Here, Projection* (Soho); *The Lucky Ones* (Hampstead); *Anthony & Cleopatra, Taming of the Shrew* (Haymarket) and *Frame 312* (Donmar Warehouse).

Film and television credits include: *New Tricks, Frankie, First Thing, The Bill, Margot, Night of the Lotus, 1408, Going Going, The Take, Doctors, Law & Order, Heartbeat, Five Days, Messiah, The Blue Borsalino, Full Time* and *Midsomer Murders*.

ROGER SLOMAN Tom

Theatre credits include: *the Magistrate, Mother Courage, Henry IV –Parts I & II, Inadmissible Evidence, Machinal* (National Theatre); *Goodbye To All That, Wholesome Glory* (Royal Court); *Danger: Memory* (Jermyn Street); *The Fairy Queen* (Glyndebourne); *2000 Feet Away, Fosdyke Saga* (Bush); *Humble Boy* (Northampton); *Henry V* (Royal Exchange Manchester); *Great Expectations, The Mandate, Much Ado About Nothing, Scenes From A Marriage, Merry Wives of Windsor* (RSC); *Loves A Luxury* (Orange Tree); *A Chorus of Disapproval* (Scarborough); *The Iceman Cometh* (Almeida); *My Night With Reg* (Criterion); *The Cherry Orchard* (Roundhouse); *Birds of Passage* (Hampstead); *What The Butler Saw* (Salisbury Playhouse); *Brassneck and Bendigo* (Nottingham Playhouse).

Film and television credits include: *eastEnders, Inside No.9, Doc Martin, Little Crackers, Shameless, Small Island, Holby City, Foyle's War, Touch Me I'm Karen Taylor, Thieves Like Us, Heartbeat, Family Business, Grass, The Cazalet Chronicles, The Vicar of Dibley, I Saw You, Crossroads, Midsomer Murders, My Family, Roger Roger, Family Affairs, The Missing Postman, Goodnight Sweetheart, Peak Practice, Richard II, Heartbeat, Time After Time, The Bill, Cracker, Wycliffe, Mike & Angelo, The Life & Times of Henry Pratt, Kevin & Co, Grace & Favour, Bottom, Danton's Death, Pennies From Heaven, Ripping Yarns, A Kick Up The Eighties, The Young Ones, Minder, Chunky Monkey, Sorted, Tenth Kingdom, Beautiful People, Beowulf, Loch Ness, Nuts In May, Young Indiana Jones, Reds, The Monster Club* and *Priest of Love*.

CREATIVE TEAM

ANNE-LOUISE SARKS (Director)
Anne-Louise works professionally as an actor, director and dramaturg. From 2013 – 2016 she was Resident Director at Belvoir. From 2010 to 2013 she was Artistic Director of The Hayloft Project and was previously a director-in-residence at Malthouse Theatre.
Belvoir credits include: *A Christmas Carol*, *Nora* (Co-Adaptor/ Director); *Medea* – Winner Sydney Theatre Award Best Direction, Best Mainstage Production and Best New Australian Work, Winner AWGIE Best Stage Play, Nominated – 2013 Helpmann Awards Best Direction, Best New Australian Work, Best Play; *Elektra/Orestes*, *Stories I Want to Tell You in Person* (Director); *The Wild Duck* (Assistant Director) and *Oedipus Schmoedipus* and *Thyestes* (Dramaturg).
Other directing credits include: *The Seed* (Melbourne Theatre Company); *The Nest, Yuri Wells, By Their Own Hands* (The Hayloft Project); *Medea* (Gate, London).

TOM SCUTT (Designer)
For the Lyric: *Fantastic Mr Fox* (Nuffield Theatres Southampton/ Curve), *Cinderella* 2012, *Mogadishu* (also Royal Exchange Manchester/UK Tour), Dick Whittington 2010, *Aladdin* 2011, *Jack and the Beanstalk* 2009.
Other theatre credits include: *king Charles III* (Almeida/Wyndham's/ Music Box, New York); *Constellations* (Royal Court/Duke of York's/ Manhattan Theatre Club) – Winner Best Set Designer WhatsOnStage Awards; *The Deep Blue Sea, Medea, 13* (National Theatre); *Jesus Christ Superstar* (Regent's Park Open Air Theatre); *Elegy, Les Liaisons Dangereuses, The Weir* (Donmar Warehouse); *A Number* (Nuffield Southampton Theatres/Young Vic); *Mr Burns, King Lear, Through A Glass Darkly, The Merchant of Venice* (Almeida); *East is East* (Trafalgar Studios/UK Tour); *Hope, The Ritual Slaughter of Gorge Mastromas, No Quarter, Remembrance Day* (Royal Court); *Absent Friends* (Harold Pinter); *South Downs/ The Browning Version* (Chichester Festival Theatre/ Harold Pinter); *On Off* (Aarhus Teater).
Opera credits include: *Wozzeck* (English National Opera); *How The Whale Became* (Royal Opera House); *The Flying Dutchman* (Scottish Opera); *Rigoletto* (Opera Holland Park).

PAULE CONSTABLE (Lighting Designer)
Paule is an Artistic Associate of the Lyric Hammersmith, the National Theatre and Matthew Bourne's *New Adventures*.
For the Lyric: *herons, Blasted, Three Sisters, The Servant, Oliver Twist.*
Other theatre credits include: *wonder.land, Behind the Beautiful Forevers, The Light Princess, Table, This House, The Curious Incident*

of the Dog in the Night-Time – Winner 2013 Olivier Award and 2015 Tony Award for Best Lighting, *War Horse* – Winner 2011 Tony Award for Best Lighting (also West End/International Tour/Broadway), *Saint Joan* – Winner Knight of Illuminations Award for Best Lighting, *His Dark Materials* – Winner 2005 Olivier Award, Best Lighting (National Theatre); *Wolf Hall* (Swan/Aldwych/Broadway); *How To Hold Your Breath*, *Clybourne Park*, *Posh* (Royal Court) and *The Red Shoes* (Matthew Bourne).

NICK MANNING (Sound Designer)
Nick is Head of Sound at the Lyric Hammersmith.
For the Lyric: *shopping & F***ing, Herons, Tipping the Velvet, Secret Theatre Company, Ghost Stories* (also Duke of York's/Liverpool Playhouse/Panasonic Theatre, Toronto/Arts Theatre), *Metamorphosis* (also UK & International Tour), *The Chair Plays, Morning, Saved*, and Roald Dahl's *Twisted Tales* (also UK Tour) *Comedians, The Birthday Party, The Resistible Rise of Arturo Ui, Beauty and the Beast, Absolute Beginners, The Odyssey, Girls Are Bigger Than Others, The Firework-Maker's Daughter, Oliver Twist, The Prince of Homburg* (also RSC), *The Servant.*
Other theatre credits include: *happy Birthday Sunita* (Rifco/Watford Palace); *Mr Swallow – The Musical* (The Invisible Dot); *Candida* (Theatre Royal Bath), *Jumpers for Goalposts* (Paines Plough/UK Tour); *The Acid Test* and *The Empire* (Royal Court); *Airsick, Crooked, When You Cure Me* (The Bush); *Gizmo Love, Excuses* and *Out of Our Heads* (ATC).

IMOGEN KNIGHT (Movement Director)
Theatre/opera credits include: *The Winter's Tale, Powder Her Face* (English National Opera); *Amadeus, The Threepenny Opera, Les Blancs, I Want My Hat Back, Edward II, Dido, Queen Of Carthage* (National Theatre); *The Emperor, Measure For Measure, Dirty Butterfly* (Young Vic); *Our Ladies Of Perpetual Succour* (National Theatre of Scotland/ National Theatre/UK Tour); *Red Velvet* (Garrick); *Linda, God Bless The Child, The Low Road, A Time To Reap* (Royal Court); *The Skriker* (Manchester International Festival/Royal Exchange Manchester); *Carmen Disruption, Little Revolution, Turn Of The Screw, King Lear, Measure For Measure, When The Rain Stops Falling* (Almeida); *Hamlet, Blindsided, Cannibals* (Royal Exchange Manchester); *In Time O'Strife, An Appointment With The Wicker Man, The Missing* (National Theatre of Scotland); *The Crucible* (The Old Vic); *Pests* (Clean Break, Royal Exchange, Royal Court/UK Tour); *The Little Sweep* (Malmo Opera).
Film and television credits include: *On Chesil Beach* (Golam Films); *Harlots* (ITV); *Call The Midwife, The Hollow Crown* (BBC).

The Drover's Wife

The Wild Duck

Angels in America

The Diary of a Madman

BELVOIR

Located in the heart of Sydney, Belvoir is one of Australia's most celebrated theatre companies. For more than thirty years, Belvoir has gathered Australia's most prominent and promising theatre artists to realise an annual season of work that is dynamic, challenging and visionary.

Belvoir is a traditional home for the great old crafts of acting and story in Australian theatre. It is a platform for voices that won't otherwise be heard. And it is a gathering of outspoken ideals. In short: theatricality, variety of life, and faith in humanity.

Every year, the company showcases new Australian plays, Indigenous works, re-imagined classics and new international writing. Audiences remember many landmark productions including *The Drover's Wife, Angels in America, Brothers Wreck, The Glass Menagerie, Neighbourhood Watch, The Wild Duck, Medea, The Diary of a Madman, Death of a Salesman, The Blind Giant is Dancing, Hamlet, Cloudstreet, Aliwa, The Book of Everything, Keating!, The Exile Trilogy, Exit the King, The Sapphires* and *Who's Afraid of Virginia Woolf?*

Today, under Artistic Director Eamon Flack and Executive Director Brenna Hobson, Belvoir tours nationally and internationally, and continues to create its own brand of rough magic for new generations of audiences.

For more information, please visit
www.belvoir.com.au

Tipping The Velvet

Bugsy Malone

Herons

A Midsummer Night's Dream

lyric

The Lyric Hammersmith is one of the UK's leading producing theatres. For more than one hundred and twenty years it has been responsible for creating some of the UK's most adventurous and acclaimed theatrical work. It has gained a national reputation for its work with and for children and young people and creates pathways into the arts for young talent from all backgrounds, helping to diversify our industry. Recent productions include the smash hit *Bugsy Malone*, the international tour and co-production with Filter Theatre of *A Midsummer Night's Dream* and a new stage adaptation of Sarah Waters' *Tipping the Velvet*.

The Lyric's dual commitment to producing the highest quality contemporary theatre, alongside nurturing the creativity of young people is what makes it unique within the cultural ecology of the UK. It is a local theatre rooted in its community with a national and international reputation for the quality and innovation of its artistic work.

In April 2015 the Lyric reopened following a multi-million pound capital project, which saw the addition of the Reuben Foundation Wing housing state-of-the-art facilities for theatre, dance, film, music, digital and more. The 'new' Lyric is now the largest creative hub in West London and home to an innovative partnership of like-minded leading arts organisations who work together to deliver life-changing creative opportunities for thousands of young West Londoners.

Artistic Director Sean Holmes
Executive Director Sian Alexander

For more information, please visit
lyric.co.uk

Supported by

Registered Charity, No. 278518

Photography by Johan Persson and Tristram Kenton

The Lyric is fully committed to reducing its impact on the environment. We have recently been awarded 4 star Creative Green certification by Julie's Bicycle for our green initiatives and a BREEAM (Building Research Establishment Environmental Assessment Method) rating of Excellent for our building.

Our building incorporates many energy saving and environmental features including a green sedum roof, natural ventilation, air-source heat pumps, LED lighting throughout and more. Plus, we recycle everything and last year saved 464 trees. For more information visit www.lyric.co.uk

LYRIC HAMMERSMITH SUPPORTERS

Thank you to all our wonderful supporters who donate to the Lyric's work on and offstage. We couldn't do it without you.

CIRCLE OF SEVENTEEN
Chris & Amanda Curry
Peter Raymond
Di & Peter Shore
Duncan & Kirsten White

LOVE THE LYRIC
Anonymous
Sian & Rob Alexander
Carrie & John Armstrong
Laura & John Banes
Lucy Bennell
Stephianne Black & Sherice Pitter
Guillaume & Carole Bonpun
Lisa Burger
The Callanan Family
Mike Dibb & Cheli Duran
Andrew & Lindsay Elder
Caroline Elliot
Liz Elston Mayhew & Luke Mayhew
Susannah Fancelli
Sadie Feast & Sean Holmes
Jane Fletcher
Kim Grant
Lynne Guyton & Nick Dale
Lesley Hill & Russ Shaw
Alex Joffe
Ann Joseph
Juliet & Michael Humphries
Joanna Kennedy
Kate McGrath
John McVittie
Emma & Michael O'Kane
Marianne Rance
Peter Raymond
Janet Robb
Cathy Robertson
Tania Tate

INDIVIDUALS
Anonymous
Kate Brooke
Chris & Amanda Curry
Roger de Freitas
Livia & Colin Firth
Nick & Allison Gaynor
John & Clare Grumbar

Sheila Clarke & Charles Gurassa
Kate & Kevin McGrath
Sheelagh O'Neill
Sandy & Caroline Orr
Caroline Posnansky
Jon & NoraLee Sedmak
Sarah Jane Stubbs
Roger & Kate Wylie

TRUST & FOUNDATIONS
Andrew Lloyd Webber Foundation
Aziz Foundation
British Council
Charles Hayward Foundation
The Charlotte Bonham-Carter Charitable Trust
The Daisy Trust
Discovery Foundation
Esmée Fairbairn Foundation
Fagus Anstruther Memorial Trust
Garfield Weston Foundation
Golsoncott Foundation
Hammersmith United Charities
The Idlewild Trust
The Ironmongers' Company
Jack Petchey Foundation
John Lyon's Charity
John Thaw Foundation
McGrath Charitable Trust
People's Postcode Trust
Reuben Foundation
Sam Griffiths Foundation
SHINE Trust
The Tudor Trust
Winton Philanthropies

COMPANIES
Barclays
Bloomberg
HammersmithLondon
MAC
Piper Private Equity
UKTV
Hotel Partner – Novotel London West

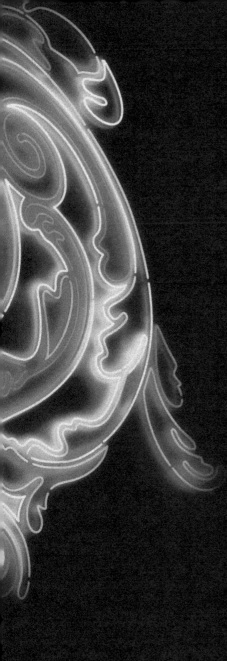

Love the Lyric

The Lyric is a registered charity, and we rely on the generous support of our Friends, Supporters, Trusts and Companies who contribute to our work. Our Public Funding provides only 25% of our running costs so for every £1 of subsidy we receive we need to earn or raise another £3.

The Lyric is West London's largest producing theatre, creating work that is provoking, entertaining, popular, eclectic, messy, contradictory and diverse.

We have one of the youngest and most diverse audiences of all UK theatres, and this diversity extends to all aspects of the Lyric, both onstage and offstage. Last year thousands of young people attended classes for acting, music, dance and film in our wonderful new Reuben Foundation Wing.

We have an 80% success rate of re-engaging disadvantaged young people into education, employment and training through our specialised theatre-based programmes.

We do hope that you will join us and be at the heart of our journey, developing the new Lyric for the next generation. There are many ways to Love the Lyric, and by supporting us you can help us continue to deliver dynamic work onstage and offstage.

WAYS TO GET INVOLVED

BECOME A FRIEND FOR £50
Join us and enjoy all that the Lyric has to offer including entertaining and innovative theatre along with special events.
Become a Lyric Friend and receive benefits including:
- 20% discount on tickets to Lyric main house shows,
- Invitations to special Friends' events,
- No ticket exchange fee,
- And more.

LOVE THE LYRIC SUPPORTERS' SCHEME
To become further involved with our work and to philanthropically support the theatre helping us to change lives, you can join as a 'Love the Lyric' supporter. From £25 per month you can enjoy benefits including access to unique and exciting events, a dedicated booking line and more insights into our work on and offstage.
- Hearts from £300 per year
- Sweethearts from £1,000 per year
- Lionhearts from £3,000 per year
- Heart & Soul from £5,000 per year

CORPORATE SUPPORT AND EVENTS
We have many opportunities for companies to engage with the Lyric. Whether it's hosting events or hiring our spaces, entertaining clients, training staff or fulfilling CSR objectives, we can create bespoke packages to meet the needs of your organisation.

REMEMBERING THE LYRIC HAMMERSMITH
You may want to remember the Lyric in your Will. Legacies left to charities are tax free and your entire gift will go directly to support the Lyric's work.

For more information on supporting the Lyric please contact the Development Team on development@lyric.co.uk or 020 8741 6822 ext. 404.

SEVENTEEN

Matthew Whittet

SEVENTEEN

OBERON BOOKS
LONDON

WWW.OBERONBOOKS.COM

First published in 2017 by Oberon Books Ltd
521 Caledonian Road, London N7 9RH
Tel: +44 (0) 20 7607 3637 / Fax: +44 (0) 20 7607 3629
e-mail: info@oberonbooks.com
www.oberonbooks.com

A catalogue record for this book is available from the British Library.

PB ISBN: 9781786820914
E ISBN: 9781786820921

Cover Design by Tom Gladstone
Photography by Jay Brooks

Printed and bound by CPI Group (UK) Ltd, Croydon, CR0 4YY.

Characters

TOM

MIKE

EMILIA

JESS

RONNY

LIZZY

A park. Dusk.

RONNY is sitting in front of a slide.

He's wearing a school uniform with only three signatures written in marker pen.

Next to him is a bag. A sleeping bag is laid out on the ground.

He stares into space.

He's bereft. Like he's trapped at the bottom of a pit.

He looks up at the top of the swing. To the cross bar.

He starts to cry.

He reaches down to his bag. He can't bring himself to do what's next.

As he slowly reaches into his bag to take something out he suddenly hears music. It's coming towards him.

He frantically grabs his stuff and hides.

TOM and MIKE come in. They're drinking beer. They have their phone plugged into a speaker playing music.

MIKE seizes the playground.

MIKE:	Yes! It's fucking ours.
TOM:	Fucking yes!
MIKE:	But what about the last question?
TOM:	I wrote about the parallels between The Tempest and euthanasia.
MIKE:	Seriously? I fucking hate you. I'm gonna fail English Lit now. BEER.
TOM:	BEER.
MIKE:	FUCKING BEER.

They drink.

TOM:	You say that every time and you get A's. You're full of shit.
MIKE:	I am not.
TOM:	You're so full of shit.

MIKE:	Last year? Economics F. Business Studies F. Biology E.
TOM:	Bullshit.
MIKE:	BEER.
TOM:	BEER.
MIKE:	BEER.
TOM:	You're a fucking twat. You always beat me at everything.
MIKE:	I've failed. I bet you any money.
TOM:	Yeah? How much?
MIKE:	Holy shit. Tom… We did it.

They can hardly take in this idea.

TOM:	We made it…? It's over…?

TOM starts laughing at the thought. He can't stop.

TOM:	Oh shit, it's over.
MIKE:	I can't… Is this actually real?
TOM:	Yeah.
MIKE:	How the fuck did this happen?

They're both laughing in shock now.

TOM:	A levels. Done.
MIKE:	No more exams. Ever again.
TOM:	…until uni.

They try and take this in for a moment.

They can't. It's too big.

TOM:	What's the first thing you're gonna do?
MIKE:	Tomorrow? Vomit. In bed. Then go back to sleep.
TOM:	No, like on results day.
MIKE:	I dunno.

TOM:	It's too fucking huge. I can't even get my head around it.
MIKE:	I'm gonna go mental, eat KFC and then suck my own dick.
TOM:	Fuck off.
MIKE:	I can actually reach you know.
TOM:	Yeah but you have to do it yourself. Like with your own mouth.

MIKE shrugs.

TOM:	Doesn't that make you gay?
MIKE:	It makes you talented.
TOM:	But it's your own dick man. Your own dick!
MIKE:	I hate that you're going. Seriously. I fucking hate it.

They both fall into a silence.

MIKE:	Monday? You couldn't wait one more week to move? You're gonna miss everything.
TOM:	I know but my dad started his new job months ago, and mum said as soon as I finished/
MIKE:	Why are you even going with your parents? You're an adult now. You could live with me and we could hang out all the time.
TOM:	I want to man. I seriously want to.
MIKE:	I can't believe I'm not gonna see you guys everyday.
TOM:	You'll see the others. And I'll visit, and you'll come visit me.
MIKE:	Fucking, whatever.

Beat.

MIKE:	It's not how all this is supposed to end.

TOM:	I just… I can't believe this is going to be the last time we do this.
MIKE:	It's fucked.

They fall into a silence.

TOM pulls out some Lynx and sprays it under his arms.

MIKE:	Nup. I can't… I'm not going there.
TOM:	Mike.
MIKE:	I'm not, 'cause tonight we are going to have the best fucking night ever.

MIKE goes to grab them a drink each. He has a big swig.

MIKE:	We're going to get shit faced.
TOM:	SHIT FACED!
MIKE:	And tomorrow we're going to sit right here, in our favourite fucking place in the whole world and watch the sun rise together. You and me. Deal?
TOM:	Deal.

Beat.

MIKE:	Where's the girls?
TOM:	I'll give them a call.
MIKE:	Hey you should go Emilia tonight.
TOM:	I would rather lick my way to the centre of the earth.

Beat.

TOM:	Chris McGowan's got the hots for her anyway.
MIKE:	You are dangerously picky my friend. No wonder you've got RSI.

LIZZY sneaks in at a distance. They don't see her.

MIKE:	Hey, did you bring my letter?
TOM:	Yeah. You?

They both take out their respective letters, swap them and start tearing them open.

TOM: I can't believe we actually remembered.

MIKE: I wasn't gonna lose it. I been waiting fucking ages for this.

They start reading.

MIKE: I was such a shit back then.

TOM: I hated when Mr Allen made us write these.

MIKE: Listen to this. 'Hey Mike. Mr Allen will never get to read this so...piss shit fuck you arse cunt head.'

TOM: Good to see you've grown up since you were 11.

MIKE: 'I hate time capsules...writing letters to yourself is stupid. When I grow up I'm gonna be famous... Tom's gonna be my manager. We'll do everything together... Don't open this until the last day of secondary school... I bet you get detention again this week.'

They both keep reading, lost in their respective letters.

MIKE is tickled by his.

TOM quietly reads his. He's struck by what's inside, but doesn't show anything.

MIKE: Jesus, my handwriting was so shit.

Beat.

MIKE: What's yours say?

TOM: Nothing.

MIKE: Bullshit. Show us.

TOM: Nah.

MIKE: Why not?

TOM: It's embarrassing.

MIKE: Just show us you twat.

As LIZZY steps a little closer, TOM notices her.

TOM:	Oh shit. It's your little sister.
LIZZY:	Hi Tom.
MIKE:	No.
LIZZY:	What?
MIKE:	Fuck off.
LIZZY:	Why?
MIKE:	'Cause I said so.
LIZZY:	Is that beer? Have you got beer? Give me a beer.
MIKE:	If you don't fuck off now I'll smash you in your head.
LIZZY:	I'll smash you in your dick.

He chases her out and she screams.

LIZZY: FUCK YOU
           MUTHERFUCKAAAAHHHHH.

As TOM follows off after them RONNY creeps out again, his bags in his arms.

He watches them run across the park.

He suddenly hears JESS and EMILIA coming the other direction.

He freaks and backs into his hiding spot again.

JESS is talking on her phone. It's a difficult conversation. She has a bottle of vodka in her hand. EMILIA has bags of crisps in her arms. She looks at the playground in disgust.

EMILIA:	Where the fuck are they? Jess?
JESS:	What … I can't…/ sorry… Mum I can't…
EMILIA:	Just hang up.
JESS:	I told you. I'm staying at Em's tonight…
EMILIA:	Jess. Hang up.
JESS:	I have no idea where it is… Where did you leave it last?

EMILIA: Don't…

JESS: Can't you find it yourself?

EMILIA: You're not going back home to help her. No fucking way.

JESS: Shut up. No. Not you. I don't…/

EMILIA: Just give me the phone.

JESS: I don't hate you… Why would I hide it?…/ Mum…

            I didn't touch it… Don't shout at me. Okay? Don't call me that… Don't fucking call me that…

EMILIA: Jess… Jess, give it to me. Jess. Just give me the phone. Jess.

EMILIA tries to take the phone.

JESS: Em, don't…

EMILIA: Mrs Goodes. Jess can't talk now. She'll call you back later.

She hangs up.

JESS: What the fuck Em?

EMILIA: There's no use talking to her when she's like that.

JESS: What else am I going to do?

EMILIA: She loses her shit. You don't deserve it.

JESS: You can't fucking do that Em! It makes things worse.

The phone starts to ring.

EMILIA: Don't answer it.

JESS: Stop telling me what to do.

EMILIA: I'm just trying to help.

The phone stops ringing.

EMILIA: Why didn't you tell me it was like this again?

JESS:	'Cause I didn't feel like it, alright?

Pause.

JESS:	She got so smashed the other morning she passed out on the kitchen floor. I didn't find her till I got home. She'd vomited everywhere.
EMILIA:	Jess.

Beat.

JESS:	She never remembers. I bet you any money she doesn't even remember it was our last exam today.
EMILIA:	You should call your aunt. You shouldn't be doing this on your own.
JESS:	Stop telling me what to do. I need you to be my friend, not my fucking counsellor.

Pause.

EMILIA pulls out a present.

EMILIA:	I know it's five hours early but…

She hands it to JESS.

JESS:	But I didn't want any presents…
EMILIA:	Eighteen's gonna be good. I know you don't want to think about it but trust me. It gets better. Alright?

JESS starts to smile.

EMILIA:	Don't worry about your mum. Not tonight. It's just about us tonight.

She opens it. It's something small. Something that means a lot to them.

JESS:	I'm getting you so smashed.
EMILIA:	I know what you're doing.
JESS:	And you're gonna snog Chris whether you like it or not.
EMILIA:	How many times I have to tell you, I'm not interested in Chris McGowan.

JESS: Who said you had to be interested?

EMILIA: He's an idiot and he's got a head the size of a grapefruit. It's way too small.

JESS: Jesus. You are such a frigid princess sometimes.

EMILIA: I am not.

JESS: No wonder you get nose bleeds.

EMILIA: I get nose bleeds because of a deviated septum.

JESS: Frigid princess.

EMILIA: That's a horrible thing to say to me. Do you know that?

JESS: Yeah but I fucking love you. Do you know that?

Beat.

JESS's phone rings, but it's a different ring tone now – a song. She moves a little to the song, teasing EMILIA with it.

EMILIA: And no. I'm not dancing either. So don't even try it.

She answers it.

JESS: Where are you?

EMILIA: Is that Mike?

JESS: We're in the spot. Where are you?

They start to head off, still on the phone.

EMILIA: I told her she should dump you tonight.

JESS: Don't worry. It's just the frigid princess.

A moment after they go RONNY appears again.

He's still carrying all his stuff.

He doesn't know what to do. He looks to where the others last walked off. He goes to leave but is sprung by a silent LIZZY who has snuck in behind him.

LIZZY: I know you. You're in my brother Mike's year.

RONNY: You scared the shit out of me.

LIZZY: What are you doing hanging out in the
             toilets?

He doesn't know what to say.

LIZZY: Were you doing a poo?

RONNY: …maybe.

LIZZY: With all your bags?

RONNY: I don't have any bags.

LIZZY: Sure you don't.

RONNY doesn't know what to say.

She hears the boys' speaker as they approach.

LIZZY: I'm watching you.

She runs off.

He hears the guys approaching. He doesn't know what to do.

He decides not to run. He throws his bags behind the toilets and immediately comes back as the boys are walking in.

RONNY: HEY GUYS!

The other two panic.

TOM: Fuck. No! Not Ronny.

MIKE: Keep walking. Go go go!

RONNY: HEY MIKE. TOM.

TOM: … Heyyyy.

Ronny   Hey how weird is that? Bumping into you
             guys.

TOM: So weird.

RONNY: I thought it was you guys. Even when you
             were way over there. I was like, 'There's my
             G's!'

MIKE: Fucking shoot me now.

RONNY squirms.

RONNY: So… Tommy. How'd you get on?

TOM:	With what?
RONNY:	English Lit.
TOM:	… Alright.
RONNY:	I bet you caned it. You're like a brain on legs. I've never met anyone as smart as you. Except maybe you Mike. But you're more like a sexy brain on legs. Not that you're not sexy as well Tommy. You're both really sexy guys…

MIKE coughs/speaks into his hand.

MIKE:	So gay.

RONNY seems not to hear.

RONNY:	…yeah, anyway… I'm pretty sure I failed it. You know me.
MIKE:	Yeah, not really.
RONNY:	English Lit has never really been my strong point.

Beat.

RONNY:	Or maths, or science, or most other subjects… so it's a good time to celebrate! 'Cause I won't when I get my results back.

The boys just stare at him. MIKE elbows TOM.

RONNY:	So… Have you guys got a big one planned?
MIKE:	No.
TOM:	Well, a small one. A really, really small one actually.
RONNY:	I saw Jess a minute ago. You guys are still going out aren't you?
MIKE:	Yeah we are. So don't get any ideas or I'll punch you in your head.
RONNY:	I wouldn't dream of it Mike. Not that I wouldn't actually dream of it. Who wouldn't!

She's well fit. Yeah, so…is anyone else coming?

TOM: … Chris. Maybe.

RONNY: Oh, Chris? He cracks me up.

TOM: Really?

RONNY: Great lad, Chris. Great lad. Small head though.

Beat.

RONNY: So, do you lads… Ummm… You lads don't mind if I just hang out do you?

The boys don't answer.

RONNY: Cause I don't really have much else planned so… But if you don't I can…

The boys look at him in silence. Neither willing to break. He gets the hint.

RONNY: Okay. That's cool. I'm cool with that. I'll umm… see you lads around I guess…

TOM: Wait. Don't go.

RONNY: Really?

TOM: Yeah. Of course you can hang out. Can't he Mike?

MIKE: You are a fuckwit.

RONNY: Really? You had me worried for a minute there.

RONNY starts to dance on the spot.

RONNY: Are you going to get some tunes happening later?

He dances a little more.

RONNY: I haven't danced in ages. I love dancing.

RONNY gets carried away with his dancing on the spot. His hips pumping like a maniac.

TOM starts to laugh at him. He can't control it.

MIKE just stares at him.

MIKE: What the fuck is that?

JESS and EMILIA come in.

JESS: LET'S GET SHIT FACED!

EMILIA: Tell me why we're here again.

RONNY stops when he realizes the girls are there.

RONNY: Hi. Emmy.

EMILIA: Who invited you?

JESS goes for one of MIKE's drinks. TOM is still laughing about RONNY's dance.

JESS: Give me one of those.

EMILIA: We're actually adults now. We could be in a fucking pub. Did you pick this spot just to piss me off?

MIKE: Your life is just one long period isn't it? You'd be useful in a maze.

EMILIA: A children's playground? Seriously? How fucking old are we?

TOM laughs again.

EMILIA: What are you laughing at you moron?

TOM: Nothing.

JESS: We always come here. You know that.

MIKE: I fucking love this place. Everything important in my life has happened in this place.

EMILIA: Oh my god, tonight's going to be all about you isn't it?

MIKE: Yeah, it is.

TOM: We should watch out for the police though.

MIKE: They are not gonna give a shit you testicle.

TOM:	They will. They'll kick us out of here. It happened to Alex last month.
EMILIA:	Alex is a moron.
JESS:	Hey Donny.
RONNY:	Ronny.
JESS:	Nice to meet you.
RONNY:	What are you talking about Jess? I'm in your year.
MIKE:	Hey. I can't wait to see you go down the slide when you're covered in your own vomit.
EMILIA:	Oh you're so funny? Let's get Emilia so drunk and watch her fall over like a spastic.
MIKE:	I reckon you've got about half an hour in you. Max.
TOM:	Guys, it's over… we've finished.
JESS:	OH MY FUCKING GOD. WE FINISHED!

They scream in celebration. MIKE sprays beer everywhere.

As the screams die down they look at each other.

They all try to take this in. It's enormous.

JESS starts to cry.

MIKE:	Stop it.

MIKE throws his arms around JESS. TOM joins in.

RONNY sees his chance and joins in from the outside.

He looks to EMILIA, motioning her in.

RONNY:	Come and get some love Emmy.

She reluctantly joins the hug.

Still in the hug JESS pulls a phone out of her pocket and holds it up.

MIKE:	What are you doing?
JESS:	This isn't happening again.

They stay in the huddle and turn to face the shot, then JESS makes them go back into the group hug.

LIZZY runs in, stopping in her tracks when she sees them. She watches them for a while. Horrified. She takes her camera out and starts to film them.

LIZZY: Oh my god, are you lot about to bum each other? Can I film it?

MIKE: GO HOME!

LIZZY: It'll just be for personal use.

MIKE runs at her and she skitters away, grabbing her side.

LIZZY: Don't! I've still got a fucking stitch.

She grabs the speaker off the ground and holds it up threateningly.

LIZZY: Touch me and I'll smash your speaker!

TOM: That's mine you psycho bitch!

MIKE heads off after LIZZY.

EMILIA: I am not frigid. Alright?

RONNY grabs the bag of crisps from EMILIA's hands and goes over to the play equipment. She tries to get them back off him.

TOM and JESS are left alone.

JESS: How the fuck did we ever become friends?

TOM: Just lucky I guess.

They both fall into a silence.

JESS: You're gonna make me cry tonight. You shit.

TOM: It's not my fault.

JESS: Why are you going? This is all too quick.

TOM: It's my parents. I don't want to go. Not yet.

JESS: But why are you even following them to Bristol? What if you don't get in there?

TOM: I'll... I'll figure something out.

JESS: It's shit. You'll go and then Em'll piss off to uni next.

TOM:	You're probably gonna go with her too though, aren't you?
JESS:	I don't know… I don't know what's happening yet.
TOM:	You'll get the grades. For sure.
JESS:	I'll probably have to stay and look after my mum anyway.
TOM:	No way. You'll get them.
JESS:	Whatever.
TOM:	Mike'll still be here.

Beat.

Her phone rings. It's her mum. TOM peers down at her phone. EMILIA calls out.

EMILIA:	Don't answer it!

JESS hangs up.

TOM:	Is that your mum?
JESS:	Yeah.
TOM:	Is everything alright?
JESS:	Don't go there.
TOM:	Sorry.
JESS:	Tonight's our night. Not hers.
TOM:	Totally.
EMILIA:	JESS.

They both share a smile.

TOM:	I wish I wasn't going.

The silence goes on a little too long between them.

EMILIA storms in, cutting him off.

EMILIA:	Don't leave me alone with him. He smells like shit.
JESS:	No he doesn't.

EMILIA: Oh my god. Personal Space. PERSONAL SPACE!

RONNY waves and tries to call them over.

RONNY: Hey guys. Watch this...

MIKE comes in with the speaker under his arm, an open bottle of booze in his hand, and a smug look on his face. It's playing a power pop number. LIZZY trails in sulkily behind him.

He starts to dance.

The music builds and so do MIKE's moves.

It's glorious.

RONNY comes in.

He starts to tap his foot. It spreads to his leg. It takes over his body.

MIKE chants.

MIKE: Go Ronny. Go Ronny. Go Go Go Ronny.

JESS starts dancing.

EMILIA doesn't.

LIZZY comes in dancing as the beat drops.

MIKE sees her and instantly starts to advance. LIZZY looks panicked. She turns to JESS, who steps in between them, protecting her.

JESS gives him a look of 'No you don't.'

LIZZY keeps dancing in celebration, giving MIKE the bird over and over in time to the music.

EMILIA still isn't dancing.

RONNY dances over to her, an enticing look in his eye. He gestures for her to join him.

EMILIA: No.

TOM sees his chance and gets up to dance with JESS.

His moves are small and understated.

He starts to loosen up a little more. He's a great dancer.

MIKE cuts in.

EMILIA goes up to TOM who's no longer dancing, offering up some crisps.

TOM declines.

RONNY takes the limelight and dances away, like he's completely taken by the music.

MIKE: WOOHOO.

He shimmies over to EMILIA.

He goes to take her hand but she swats him away.

EMILIA: No! I said no!

RONNY: C'mon.

He tries to take her hand again but she snaps.

EMILIA: Fuck off! Just fuck off will you!

Beat.

RONNY takes it on the chin and keeps dancing.

The song changes.

They hang out.

As the others muck around, get booze, play on the swings, etc. TOM and EMILIA watch on.

She offers up some crisps.

TOM begrudgingly takes one.

EMILIA: So. Are you looking forward to it?

TOM: What? The Dorito?

EMILIA: Bristol you idiot.

TOM: I suppose.

EMILIA: You'll do well there. Plenty of your kind.
                 Almost gifted.

TOM: Thanks.

          Pause.

TOM: I'm going to miss this.

EMILIA: What?

TOM: This. Hangin' out.

Pause.

TOM: Do you reckon we'll do this when we're older? That we'll have friends who we can just chill out and talk and stare into space with?

EMILIA: I hope not.

TOM: Seriously? I do.

EMILIA: Why?

TOM: I dunno... It's like everything makes sense when we all just do nothing. You know what I mean?

EMILIA: No. Not really.

Beat.

TOM: We're only going to be young once and we're only going to have more responsibility. Not less. And when we all do this, I feel free. Like the things I get stressed about get easier. Is that specific enough for you?

EMILIA: I suppose.

They both fall into their own thoughts for a moment.

TOM: You excited about uni?

EMILIA: Yeah. It'll be nice to be around intelligent people for a change.

TOM: Right. Thanks.

EMILIA: You're welcome.

Pause.

EMILIA: What about regrets? You got any regrets?

TOM: Talking to you now?

EMILIA: Don't be a smartarse.

TOM: Well I am only 'almost gifted'...

EMILIA: I'm serious.

TOM: Regrets?

Beat.

TOM: I don't know…

He thinks about this for a moment.

TOM: This sounds stupid, but sometimes I wish… I was more like Mike.

EMILIA: What? Like a dick?

TOM: No, more…like a man.

EMILIA: That is actually one of the stupidest things I've ever heard.

TOM: No one ever sees me like that.

EMILIA: Yes they do.

TOM: They don't! They look at me like I'm still a boy. Like I wouldn't have a bad thought in my head.

EMILIA: And that's what it means to be a man is it?

TOM: You know what I mean.

EMILIA: I'm sorry, I don't.

TOM: I just… I wish people would take me more seriously. I wish I had the balls to just go out and… do shit, you know.

EMILIA: Like what?

TOM: … I don't know…ignore me. I'm just being stupid.

Beat.

EMILIA: If it makes you feel better I think you're much more of a man than Mike will ever be.

They both fall in a silence for a moment as the others laugh.

As he looks off to them she watches him. Like she wants to say something. Just as she's about to he catches her.

TOM: What's that look?

EMILIA:	Nothing.
TOM:	You looked completely different then. It's like your whole face changed.
EMILIA:	No it didn't…
TOM:	Yeah it did. You gonna cry?
EMILIA:	Don't be stupid.
TOM:	I know what I saw.
EMILIA:	I can't help my face.
TOM:	No, that's true.
EMILIA:	Don't be an arsehole.
TOM:	I didn't mean it like that.
EMILIA:	Well how did you mean it then?

Beat.

TOM:	I dunno… Not like that.

Beat.

TOM:	Not like that Em.

EMILIA storms off towards JESS and the others.

TOM is left alone. He takes the letter out of his pocket and looks at it. He gets lost in thought for a moment.

MIKE sneaks up and snatches the letter from TOM's hand.

TOM:	No, Mike. Don't!

RONNY listens in, LIZZY not far behind.

MIKE:	'Dear future Tom,'
TOM:	Give it back.
MIKE:	'Hi. Remember me? It's Tom. I'm about to turn 12, and you should have just finished your A levels.'
LIZZY:	Oh my god that's like cute time travel!
MIKE:	'Is Mike still your best friend? Do you have any muscles yet?'

TOM: Don't be a prick.

MIKE: 'Do you still have weird dreams? I had one
          last night about a monkey riding a pig. It was
          well freaky. I have no idea what it means.'

LIZZY: It means you're fucked in the head.

MIKE: 'I wish I was cooler. I wish I wasn't such a
          loser sometimes. Don't be like me. When I'm
          your age, if there's something you really need
          to do, you should just do it. No matter what.
          Cause if you don't you might regret it forever.'

Beat.

MIKE: 'Like if I don't go to the toilet right now. It's
          not going to be pretty, and I'll get a new
          nickname that I don't want. Keep working
          out. I want muscles. Bye. Tom.'

*TOM finally grabs the letter, quickly putting it away in his pocket.
LIZZY laughs again.*

TOM: You're an arsehole.

MIKE: What's your problem man?

TOM: I didn't fucking read yours out loud.

RONNY: I think it's great Tommy. Especially the going
          to the toilet bit. Good advice.

JESS: Was that your letter? I completely forgot
          about mine.

TOM: You're a prick.

MIKE pulls his own letter out.

MIKE: Jesus. Read mine out loud if it makes you
          feel better. I don't give a shit.

LIZZY snatches it from his hands.

LIZZY: I'll read it.

EMILIA and JESS come over with plastic cups.

EMILIA: Shots. We're doing shots.

JESS: Now we're fucking talking!

EMILIA: C'mon. Hurry up!

They grab a drink each.

MIKE: Ready?

RONNY: Yep.

JESS: Yep.

TOM: Yep.

LIZZY: Where's mine?

MIKE: Go.

They all drink except LIZZY.

LIZZY: Arsehole.

JESS: That's disgusting.

MIKE: Beer.

MIKE grabs beers and passes them around.

EMILIA: I don't know what all the fuss is about. You lot are as weak as piss.

RONNY: Take it easy Emmy. It can tend to creep up on you.

MIKE: Down in one!

They down their beers.

MIKE: So what are you idiots going to miss the most?

JESS: You calling us idiots all the time.

EMILIA: Free periods on Wednesday afternoons. Debating society.

TOM: Seriously? I fucking hate debating.

EMILIA: Mrs Frankenbaum.

MIKE: Frankenbaum? Who smells like something crept up her Frankenbaum and died years ago?

MIKE and TOM high five.

JESS:	Totally. She smells like an animal died.
MIKE:	In her arse.
JESS:	And had shitty babies.
MIKE:	That also died in her arse. Before slowly crawling into her gob.
RONNY:	Wow. That's graphic.
EMILIA:	Fuck off. They're my happy memories. Don't ruin them.
MIKE:	With stinking shit dead animal arse stories?
RONNY:	I'll miss the tree next to the cricket nets.
EMILIA:	The Wisteria! I love the Wisteria.
RONNY:	Especially in summer.
EMILIA:	I never thought about that tree. Oh god, I'm going to miss it too.
JESS:	I'm going to miss you lot…

JESS starts to cry.

MIKE:	Stop it, will you.
JESS:	I'm going to miss you lot so much.
TOM:	Me too.
MIKE:	This is not fucking happening. Change the subject. Ronny, put something on.

RONNY heads over to the speaker and changes the song.

EMILIA:	So what else are we going to do?
MIKE:	What do you mean?
EMILIA:	Tonight. What else are we going to do?
MIKE:	Drink.
EMILIA:	That's it? Seriously? For the next 7 and half hours?
JESS:	Pace yourself babe.
LIZZY:	Tom could show us his muscles.

TOM:	Shut up fucktard.
MIKE:	That's your first warning tonight. You get two more.
LIZZY:	Get fucked.
MIKE:	Only one left. Better use it wisely.
JESS:	Tom. What did your letter say?
EMILIA:	I didn't even have to read mine. I remember it word for word.
LIZZY:	You are such a freak.
EMILIA:	How old are you Lizzy?
LIZZY:	15.
MIKE:	Liar.
LIZZY:	… In a few weeks…months…later next year…
EMILIA:	You know you're just like me when I was 14.
LIZZY:	Awww! That's not nice!
EMILIA:	No, you are. I can see it in your face. You're smart.
LIZZY:	I'll give you that.
EMILIA:	You know more than anyone thinks.
LIZZY:	No.
EMILIA:	Did you know my parents told me to stop calling them mum and dad when I turned 12. They wanted me to think more like an adult, and not get stuck thinking like a stupid kid.
LIZZY:	Our dad's name is Dick…
EMILIA:	So I did, and I started planning. What A levels I'd take, what grades I'd get, what university I'd go to. Dream big Lizzy. Cause no one else is gonna to do it for you.
MIKE:	Or in your case to you.
JESS:	I would. She's hot.

RONNY:	Don't Mikey, I think it's great. I wish my parents did that sort of thing. It means they care.
EMILIA:	Thanks Ronny, but I don't need you to stand up for me. I know how to deal with dicks like him. With grace and intelligence. Two things he doesn't have in his arsenal.
MIKE:	No but I've got a few other things up my arsenal.

MIKE and TOM high five again.

JESS:	Like shit comebacks?
EMILIA:	I know how smart you are Lizzy. Don't throw it away. And don't ever let arseholes like him tell you any different.
LIZZY:	Is she drunk already?
EMILIA:	Don't be stupid! This is having no effect on me whatsoever.
LIZZY:	What are you going to do next year?
JESS:	Me? I dunno yet.
EMILIA:	Yes you do. You're going to uni with me.
JESS:	It depends. I've got options.
EMILIA:	You're not fucking hairdressing. I'm not letting you.
JESS:	It's up to you is it?
EMILIA:	You're too smart for that.
JESS:	So hairdressers are dumb yeah?
MIKE:	I want free haircuts.
JESS:	Oh now you decide to back me up?
MIKE:	Only if you're good at it though.
JESS:	You're such a cunt.
MIKE:	No one wants a bad haircut. Seriously. Not even a free one.

EMILIA:	I can't believe you're even thinking about it.
JESS:	Yeah well maybe I won't have a choice.
LIZZY:	Well, take away like uni and…hairdressing and stuff. What else? If you could do anything. What would it be? Doesn't matter how much it costs.

Beat.

JESS:	…go travelling…on my own.
MIKE:	On your own?
JESS:	What's wrong with that?
TOM:	Where would you go?
JESS:	I don't know… I'd start in Mexico maybe. Then just wing it.
MIKE:	Mexico?
JESS:	Can you stop being such a prick?
LIZZY:	I'm going to become an actress.
EMILIA:	Don't do that.
LIZZY:	But I'm good at it.
EMILIA:	Don't. It's not worth it.
JESS:	You should Lizzy. You should do what you love.
EMILIA:	Like hairdressing?
LIZZY:	Well I'm not going to work for my dad. Not like him.
MIKE:	This is supposed to be a party. Why are we talking about this shit?
JESS:	What about you Donny?
RONNY:	Ronny…
JESS:	What are you doing next year?
RONNY:	Oh you know…stuff.
JESS:	What kind of stuff?

RONNY shrugs. He doesn't know what to say.

LIZZY: Well whatever it is, he's packed and ready to go. Aren't you mate?

RONNY: Hey, who's got a special trick?

EMILIA: Don't change the subject.

RONNY: I'm not. I just want to know who's got a special trick? Something only they can do.

They all fall silent.

RONNY: C'mon. There must be something.

TOM: No.

MIKE: I got nothing.

RONNY: I don't believe you.

MIKE: What about you then?

RONNY: Me?

RONNY thinks about it for a moment.

RONNY: Alright.

RONNY does something that only he can do. An idiosyncratic trick.

They all fall over laughing.

RONNY: Good huh?

JESS: That is brilliant.

RONNY: Thanks. I've been working on it for a while.

EMILIA: Jess can pole dance.

JESS: Em? What the fuck?

TOM: Seriously?

MIKE: Why did I never know this?

EMILIA: That bit from the music video. Remember?

JESS: You twat. That's not pole dancing.

EMILIA: Whatever. Do it. It's great.

JESS: Only if you do it too.

EMILIA: Alright.

JESS: Seriously?

EMILIA: Ronny, put something on.

RONNY puts a song on.

LIZZY chants.

LIZZY: Do it. Do it. Do it.

JESS and EMILIA get up.

They stand there for a moment listening to the music.

They start to do the dance. EMILIA only gets a few moves in and freaks out. She pulls out leaving JESS to do it alone. She doesn't do too much. Just a teaser.

JESS: That's all you get.

It finishes. They all whistle and clap.

EMILIA: See what I mean? You're amazing. Tom, isn't she amazing?

TOM: …amazing.

MIKE: Yeah, she was about as sexy as diarrhea.

JESS: Fuck you.

EMILIA: Don't be an arsehole. What have you done yet? Nothing! Put your money where your mouth is.

MIKE: Speaking of putting things where your mouth is, where's Chris McGowan? Isn't he supposed to be here by now?

EMILIA: Don't change the subject.

MIKE: I wish he could see you. You're looking so hot right now.

RONNY: Tommy, you should sing something.

TOM: …I'm not very good.

EMILIA: He's right. He's quite average actually.

RONNY: You're great. I love it when you sing.

MIKE:	Yeah Tommy. I love it when you sing too. You're so amazing.
TOM:	Fuck off.
LIZZY:	Do it, or I'll hit you in your face.

TOM reluctantly gets up and starts to sing something. Something beautiful.

As he finishes they all fall into an awed silence.

RONNY:	Wow.
JESS:	That was so beautiful.
MIKE:	Yeah, but can he suck his own cock?
TOM:	I can't. I've tried.
EMILIA:	You! Enough! Do something interesting. Now.
MIKE:	Well, if you put it like that!
JESS:	Ignore him Tom. That was really beautiful.
TOM:	Thanks.
EMILIA:	C'mon. I want to see something.
MIKE:	Alright then. Truth or dare.
TOM:	Truth or Dare?
EMILIA:	That's not a special trick.
LIZZY:	But I haven't done my trick yet!
MIKE:	Scared of playing are you?
EMILIA:	No. I've got nothing to hide.
RONNY:	Who's first?
MIKE:	Me. Tom?
TOM:	No. I don't want to.
MIKE:	Go on. And no lying. I know when you lie.
RONNY:	Oh I'm terrible at lying! I'm going to be terrible at this game.
LIZZY:	That's the point Ronny.

RONNY:	Oh good. Maybe I'll win.
MIKE:	So. Truth or dare?

Beat.

TOM:	Truth.
MIKE:	Are you sure you want to do that?
TOM:	Just do it.
MIKE:	Right... and this is a serious question... how many times have you wanked in public?
TOM:	...define public.
MIKE:	Not in your bedroom... or bathroom... or home. Not at home. At School. Or on public transport.
TOM:	Never.
MIKE:	Liar!
TOM:	Next.
MIKE:	No way. You don't get off that easily.
JESS:	Obviously not.

JESS and EMILIA fist bump.

TOM:	Next!
LIZZY:	Me. I want to go next.
MIKE:	You're not allowed to speak anymore. You're done.
JESS:	Truth or dare?
LIZZY:	Yes!
MIKE:	Oi. I'm doing this. Truth or dare?
LIZZY:	Dare.
MIKE:	Do ten star jumps on the spot.
LIZZY:	Seriously?
MIKE:	Naked.

Beat.

TOM:	She's your sister!
LIZZY:	No.
MIKE:	She wanted to play. If she can't stand the heat…
LIZZY:	I'm not doing that.

LIZZY walks out.

MIKE:	And now she's gone. You can all thank me later.
JESS:	LIZZY, DON'T GO.
TOM:	COME BACK.
LIZZY:	*(Off.)* I'M NOT DOING THAT. I'M DOING THIS! WOOHOO!

LIZZY starts to strip in the distance.

JESS:	What the fuck?
TOM:	Oh shit! Oh shit man!
RONNY:	Wow. That came off quick.
LIZZY:	*(Off.)* HOW DO I LOOK FROM OVER HERE MIKEY!
JESS:	YOU LOOK FUCKING AMAZING!
LIZZY:	WOOHOO! 1. 2. 3. 4. 5/
MIKE:	Tell when it's over will you?
JESS:	GO LIZZY!
LIZZY:	*(Off.)* /6. 7. 8. 9. 10.
JESS:	I LOVE YOU LIZZY.
LIZZY:	*(Off.)* FUCK YOU VERY MUCH.
JESS:	YOU ARE THE BEST!

LIZZY heads back in pulling her clothes back on.

MIKE:	Whatever.
LIZZY:	NEXT.
MIKE:	Emilia.

EMILIA:	What?
MIKE:	Truth or dare?
EMILIA:	Truth.
MIKE:	If you had to fuck one of us here right now, who would it be?
EMILIA:	Dare.
MIKE:	You can't change mid game.
EMILIA:	I don't care. Dare.
JESS:	Just let her.
MIKE:	Alright. Kiss Tom. Full tongue.
TOM:	Hang on.
EMILIA:	I'm not doing that.
LIZZY:	I'll do it.
MIKE:	I know Chris McGowan's not here, but he'll do. Otherwise you're out of the game and you'll have to piss off forever.
JESS:	Mike, don't.
EMILIA:	No.
MIKE:	I know his head's not as small as Chris's but/
JESS:	Stop it!

EMILIA starts to go green from too much drink.

MIKE:	Just close your eyes and imagine your tongue in Chris's tiny mouth instead.
JESS:	Leave her alone.
MIKE:	Actually, why isn't Chris here? Do you think it could have something to do with the fact you're such a fucking uptight bitch?
JESS:	What did you just say?
MIKE:	Here we go. What are you, my fucking mother?
JESS:	No. I'm your fucking girlfriend!

TOM:	What's wrong with you?
MIKE:	I'm just joking! She's much better looking than my mother. But her mother? Now that's fucked up.

JESS storms off.

TOM:	You're being a complete arsehole.
MIKE:	And you all take things too seriously. I need a piss.

MIKE heads towards the toilets, to where RONNY hid his bags.

RONNY jumps up.

RONNY:	Mikey! Not those ones… they're broken.

RONNY steers MIKE away from the toilets and they head off into the bushes.

EMILIA:	Ugh.
TOM:	Are you alright?
EMILIA:	I'm not feeling so great…

EMILIA starts to walk off. LIZZY follows.

LIZZY:	Is she going to vomit? I think she's going to vomit. Are you going to vomit?
EMILIA:	No…

LIZZY gets out her phone to film her and starts to make vomiting sounds. EMILIA heads off even faster.

They're gone.

TOM is alone.

He takes out the letter and looks at it for a moment. He takes a deep breath.

JESS storms back in and he puts it away quickly.

JESS:	Where is he? He can't speak to me like that.
TOM:	I know.

JESS:	I've fucking had it Tom. I'm not taking his shit anymore. I get it at home from Mum. I get it from him. I get it from Em. I'm sick of it.
TOM:	You should be.
JESS:	I'm gonna smack him in the head tonight if he says anything else.
TOM:	Fuck yeah.
JESS:	You're going to back me up?
TOM:	I'll try.
JESS:	You better.
TOM:	I will.

Beat.

TOM:	It's tonight. He's in a weird mood cause of finishing and everything.
JESS:	Don't make excuses. He's been like this for ages.
TOM:	I guess.

Pause.

JESS:	It's like… I'm about to turn 18 tomorrow.
TOM:	What the fuck? Are you serious?
JESS:	I didn't want to tell anyone.
TOM:	Why not?
JESS:	Just 'cause. But my point is that I'm only gonna be 18 but I feel like I can already see how everything's going to go. Like for the next 40 years if I'm not careful. I'll stay at home, look after Mum, look after Mike… I can fucking see it coming.
TOM:	Don't say that.
JESS:	But I can.
TOM:	You could do anything you wanted.

JESS:	Now you're starting to sound like Em.
TOM:	Yeah, but she's right.
JESS:	I just… Argghh…
TOM:	What?
JESS:	I'm sorry… I'm drunk Tom. I don't want to dump all this on you.
TOM:	I don't mind, really. Keep dumping.

Beat.

JESS:	It's just… I dunno, I just feel like I'm stuck. Like I'm not…

Beat.

JESS:	I just don't know what I want yet.
TOM:	That's okay isn't it?
JESS:	But I do know that I need to work it out myself. You know? For myself.
TOM:	That makes total sense.
JESS:	Does it?

Beat.

JESS:	Fuck it. What am I doing? I said I wasn't going there tonight.
TOM:	You shouldn't.
JESS:	Exactly. Tonight's tonight. It's not tomorrow.
TOM:	Actually in about half an hour…
JESS:	Don't tell anyone.

EMILIA calls from off.

EMILIA:	*(Off.)* JESS. JESS I NEED YOU.
JESS:	Whose idea was it to get her drunk?
TOM:	Yours.
EMILIA:	*(Off.)* JESS!!!! PLEASE!!! I'M GONNA BE SICK!!!!

Beat.

JESS:　　　　　　　I better go.

She gets up to leave and TOM stops her.

TOM:　　　　　　　…Jess. Can I show you something?

He reaches into his pocket and pulls out the letter to himself.

TOM:　　　　　　　It's my letter. From earlier… Anyway, I really… I just want you to read it.

EMILIA:　　　　　*(Off.)* I CAN'T GET UP!!!! JESS???

JESS:　　　　　　　I'LL BE THERE IN A MINUTE.

She takes out the letter and starts reading.

TOM:　　　　　　　Do it later if you want…

JESS:　　　　　　　No. She can wait.

He stands there awkwardly while she reads.

She laughs as she reads to herself.

She looks up at him.

JESS:　　　　　　　Muscles?

TOM:　　　　　　　Whatever.

She finishes reading the letter.

JESS:　　　　　　　That's funny. I used to have weird dreams too.

TOM:　　　　　　　Yeah?

JESS:　　　　　　　When I was a kid.

EMILIA:　　　　　*(Off.)* JESS?

Pause.

TOM:　　　　　　　Mine have been intense lately. Really crazy. I don't know about you, but ever since we started our exams they've been so weird.

　　　　　　　　　　But I had this one the other night… I can't stop thinking about it.

Beat.

43

I was old. In my dream I woke one morning and I'd become old. It was like my entire life had passed by in one night and I didn't know what had happened. Where it went. It was so weird. I wasn't scared. I didn't even give a shit. It was just how things were. It just happened.

I had no idea where I was. I don't think it was my bedroom. I don't think it was even my house. I called out to my mum and dad. But then I realized that they weren't around anymore. That they would have died ages ago. And I wanted to cry. So I did. I cried for what felt like years, for all the time they'd been gone, and because I never got to say goodbye. But then that finished. And I was okay. It was like I'd cried everything out of my body. Like I was totally empty.

So I started walking around this house. I had no idea where I was. I saw pictures on the walls. Of kids. Little kids. Three year olds, four year olds. And I thought… who the hell are they? I don't recognize any of them. And then it hit me. Oh god, are they mine? I'm not old enough to have kids am I? But then I realised that they couldn't have been my kids… they were probably my grandkids.

And then someone called my name.

Someone upstairs.

So I went up.

I went into another bedroom and there, sitting on the end of the bed… was you.

You weren't young anymore either. You were just like me.

And we sat there. We tried to talk about what was happening. But we couldn't. We couldn't find the words.

So we just sat.

We weren't scared.

And I loved you so much.

I was so in love with you.

I am.

Pause.

TOM: I was never going to say a word. To you or anyone. I was going to lock it all away and never think about it again… But I can't.

And when you looked at me before… when I was singing… I knew that if I didn't say something now, the moment would be gone…and I'd regret it for the rest of my life.

They both sit in silence for a while.

JESS: How long have you felt like this?

TOM: Honestly?

She nods.

TOM: A while.

EMILIA: *(Off.)* JESS. I NEED YOU.

Pause.

TOM: I'm sorry. I shouldn't have said anything. I should have just kept my mouth shut.

They sit in silence for a moment.

JESS leans over and kisses him.

It takes him completely by surprise.

They finish and look at each other.

Neither knows what to say.

TOM: What the fuck?

45

They both fall into another silence.

They kiss again.

RONNY walks in and sees them. He freezes.

She can't help smiling at TOM.

JESS: You're going in two days.

TOM: I'm going in two days.

He holds her hand tight in his.

TOM: I don't want to go now…

RONNY starts to back away and they notice him.

They all stare at each other in stunned silence.

RONNY: Emilia's calling for you…

RONNY takes off, back to the others.

JESS: Ronny?

TOM: Shit…

Neither of them knows what to do.

TOM: We should go over.

She takes his hands.

JESS: Not yet. C'mon.

They head off together in the opposite direction.

MIKE comes in, walking through the playground.

He's trying to cool off.

LIZZY comes in and stands at a distance.

MIKE: What do you want Lizzy?

LIZZY: I'm not Lizzy. I'm a ninja.

MIKE doesn't respond.

LIZZY: This is merely a disguise. I just choose when
                   I want to reveal myself.

MIKE: Right. So who are you really then?

LIZZY: I can't tell you. Otherwise I'd have to kill
            you.

Beat.

LIZZY: Who am I kidding? I wouldn't kill you. I'd
            just slap you around a bit.

MIKE: Lizzy… Can you just piss off now?

LIZZY: I could… But the problem is you wouldn't
            be able to tell if I did.

MIKE is losing patience.

LIZZY: I'd probably just become a tree. I'm that
            good.

MIKE: Just fuck off.

LIZZY: I don't want to.

MIKE: Why not?

LIZZY: Just 'cause.

Pause.

LIZZY: Are you alright?

MIKE: Don't I seem alright to you?

LIZZY: No.

MIKE: Why?

LIZZY: You look unhappy.

Beat.

LIZZY: Are you unhappy?

He does a huge fake smile.

MIKE: How's that?

LIZZY: I'm going to have nightmares now.

MIKE: Good.

LIZZY: Are you going to break up with Jess tonight?

MIKE: What?

47

LIZZY: 'Cause I reckon you don't seem happy going out with her anymore.

MIKE doesn't respond.

LIZZY: Which is weird 'cause Jess is way better than you. Like I'm totally surprised she even went out with you in the first place. She's so out of your league. Like a good eight or nine divisions. You're like almost in the Vauxhall Conference but she's heading for the Champions League. Funny. Great brain. Amazing people skills. So fucking sexy. I'd turn for her. Seriously.

MIKE: Lizzy… why are you here?

LIZZY: Well, it's a long story, but a couple of years after you were born, Mum and Dick got drunk, Dick got his dick out/

MIKE: Stop being a smart arse.

LIZZY: Easier said than done.

MIKE: Why are you here?

Beat.

LIZZY: 'Cause I'm worried… about you. I know you think I'm an idiot, but I'm not. I know what's going on.

MIKE: Oh you do, do you? What's going on then?

LIZZY: I'm not going to say it!

MIKE: You're full of shit.

LIZZY: I just don't want you to do anything stupid, that's all. I'm worried that you're going to get smashed and do something stupid.

MIKE: Just go home.

LIZZY: Is it cause you don't want to finish school?

MIKE: Lizzy…

LIZZY: Or cause Tom's leaving? Or is it something else?

Pause.

LIZZY: I've known you for ages. As long as I can remember. Literally. And in that time I've seen, I reckon, almost everything there is to know about you... But I've never seen you like this. And I reckon I know why.

Pause.

He goes to leave.

LIZZY: Mike!

MIKE: What?

LIZZY: Please. Don't...

MIKE: What? What? What?

MIKE storms off, and LIZZY watches him go.

She heads off after him.

The park in stillness for a moment.

EMILIA staggers in, followed closely behind by RONNY.

EMILIA: ... Water... I need water...

She stops.

RONNY: Are you gonna vomit again?

EMILIA: Don't!

She takes some deep breaths.

RONNY: Whatever you do, don't think about fish... or milk...or oysters...or ashtrays. They make it worse.

EMILIA stares down RONNY.

RONNY: And definitely don't think of them mixed together. In a cup. I made that mistake once.

JESS comes in.

JESS: What were you screaming about?

49

EMILIA:	Where were you?
JESS:	I wasn't far.
EMILIA:	Oh god… you never said this would happen…
JESS:	You just drank too quickly that's all.
EMILIA:	I'm going to die…
JESS:	You'll be fine. Just breath.
EMILIA:	I'm going to die…!
JESS:	Get her some water Ronny.

RONNY grabs an empty cup, and heads off to get some water as TOM arrives.

EMILIA:	You shouldn't have left me alone.
JESS:	It would've happened anyway.
EMILIA:	No it wouldn't. It's all your fault.
JESS:	Stop being a hypochondriac.

JESS and EMILIA sit together.

JESS:	Better?
EMILIA:	This whole night is a disaster.
JESS:	At least the police didn't kick us out.
EMILIA:	If they did I'd be home in bed by now and not completely humiliated.
JESS:	Just take a few deep breaths.

EMILIA does. She seems to calm a bit.

EMILIA:	I hate this Jess. I hate this so much.
JESS:	Toughen up princess.
EMILIA:	I'm not talking about being drunk.

EMILIA goes to say why but she can't.

EMILIA:	… Can you ask him to go? Just for a minute.

JESS doesn't know where this is going, but looks to TOM. He takes the hint.

JESS: Tom?

TOM: Yeah. Sure.

TOM goes.

JESS: What's going on?

Pause.

EMILIA: I… I don't know what to do…

JESS: About what?

Pause.

EMILIA: What do people think of me?

JESS: What do you mean?

EMILIA: What do they think? Tell me.

JESS: … That you're smart. That you know what you want. You're one of the most loyal friends ever.

EMILIA: I sound like a fucking Alsatian!

JESS: But you've also got an enormous heart. Why are you asking me all this? What's going on?

Pause.

EMILIA: I feel like such an idiot.

Pause.

EMILIA: Jess…there's someone I like…and I have for ages… I feel so fucking stupid even saying this!

Beat.

JESS: Is it Chris McGowan?

EMILIA: No. I don't fucking like Chris McGowan.

Beat.

JESS: Do I know them?

EMILIA: What do you think?

She can hardly say it.

EMILIA: … It's Tom.

Beat.

JESS:	… Why are you only just telling me this now?
EMILIA:	Because I couldn't before. I felt stupid even thinking about it.
JESS:	Okay.
EMILIA:	I can't believe you never saw it.
JESS:	Me neither.
EMILIA:	I dropped enough hints over the years…

Beat.

JESS:	Em…
EMILIA:	I'm not a frigid princess, okay? I'm not.
JESS:	Em… we need to/…

MIKE comes barrelling in.

MIKE:	WHERE'S THE FUCKING TEQUILA?

TOM trails behind him, unsuccessful in his attempt to stop him.

He spots JESS and EMILIA together.

MIKE:	What were you two talking about?
JESS:	Nothing.
MIKE:	Bullshit. Em. What was she telling you?
EMILIA:	That you're an idiot.
MIKE:	Tequila! Who's in?

MIKE grabs the bottle of Tequila.

LIZZY:	Me!
EMILIA:	Oh god…
MIKE:	Remember when you and me did this two years ago Tom? And you vomited in your backpack.
TOM:	I can't touch that stuff anymore.
MIKE:	That was the best fucking night ever.

MIKE pushes the bottle at TOM.

TOM: I don't feel like it.

MIKE: Drink.

TOM drinks.

MIKE: Why is there no music on? C'mon, we're
                supposed to be celebrating you dickheads!

MIKE searches for a song.

He finds the one he's after and puts it on. He starts to dance.

MIKE: C'mon. Fucking dance.

He grabs JESS and tries to get her dancing. LIZZY joins in.

MIKE: C'mon.

JESS: I don't like this song.

MIKE: I don't care.

LIZZY: I like it!

He pushes the bottle at TOM again.

MIKE: This is our last night together. We made a
                deal remember?

TOM: But I don't like Tequila.

MIKE: Jesus! What the fuck is your problem?

TOM: What's your problem?

Beat.

MIKE: You know what? I'm not letting you leave.
                And then you'll be stuck here forever. Just
                like me.

TOM: You're not stuck here. You don't have to
                work for your dad if you don't want to.

LIZZY: Yes he does.

MIKE: You think I'm talking about work? I'm not
                talking about work. I'm talking about right
                now! This park!

TOM: What do you mean?

MIKE keeps dancing to the music a little more.

MIKE:	God I love this bit.

Pause.

JESS and TOM catch each other's eye.

TOM:	Hey, we should go for a walk.
MIKE:	Can't. Dancing.
TOM:	C'mon… I need to talk to you about something.
MIKE:	Is this their plan? To get rid of me so the frigid princess can keep on bitching about me?

EMILIA gives him a filthy look.

MIKE stops dancing.

MIKE:	Don't tell me you're still pissed off about before?
EMILIA:	Every time you open your mouth you piss me off.

MIKE glares at her for a moment.

MIKE:	Hey. You know what we should do? We should play truth or dare!
JESS:	No.
MIKE:	Yes! TRUTH OR DARE! LET'S FUCKING DO IT!

A torchlight flashes through.

LIZZY:	Police!
TOM:	What?… POLICE? POLICE!!!

They all scatter except MIKE who yells.

MIKE:	FUCK YOU. FUCKING PIGS!

He throws the bottle towards the light and runs too.

RONNY:	*(Off.)* OW!

RONNY wanders in with a flashlight, and his hand clutched to his head. The bottle hit him.

RONNY:	I got your water Emmy?
EMILIA:	Ronny! You're bleeding.
RONNY:	Am I?
EMILIA:	Are you okay? Should I get you something?
RONNY:	No… I'll be fine.
EMILIA:	Come here. Let me have a look.

EMILIA sits RONNY down and using the water he brought her, she starts to clean up the cut on his head.

RONNY:	You don't have to do this. I'm fine.
EMILIA:	Shut up. You've looked after me tonight. I can look after you.
RONNY:	Thanks.

She washes the blood off.

RONNY:	You're a good person Emmy. You know that?
EMILIA:	You're drunk.
RONNY:	No, I'm not. I'm not even close. Hanging out with you lot tonight…it's meant everything to me.
EMILIA:	That's nice of you Ronny, but you have a head injury. Tonight has been a fucking disaster.
RONNY:	No it hasn't.

Beat.

RONNY:	Not yet anyway.
EMILIA:	You know, I really thought getting smashed would help. That it'd give me courage. But did it? No. It's just turned everything to shit.
RONNY:	What are you saying? You're the most courageous person I've ever met.
EMILIA:	Well, why am I so fucking hopeless when it comes to the one thing I want? I'm sick

of having secrets Ronny. I hate them. From now on no more secrets.

Pause.

RONNY's mind is spinning. He is holding so much in.

RONNY: I know you lot didn't want me here tonight.

EMILIA: That's not true.

RONNY: Yes it is.

Beat.

RONNY: I know everyone can't stand me. Everyone thinks I'm a weirdo.

EMILIA: That's not true Ronny.

RONNY: Yes it is Em. But tonight... I feel different. I feel like for the first time in forever I've just been able to be me... And that's why I can't be the person who stuffs it all up...

Beat.

RONNY: 'Cause it wasn't my fault that I saw them.

EMILIA: Saw who?

Beat.

RONNY: Mikey is going to be so upset.

EMILIA stares at him. She can't quite believe her ears.

RONNY: You can't say anything... but I saw Jess...

Beat.

EMILIA: ...and Tom?

He nods.

Pause.

RONNY: They were snogging.

EMILIA: What?

Pause.

EMILIA: What the fuck??

| RONNY: | Please Emmy. You can't say anything. You have to promise me you won't say anything. |

She turns and races off towards the others.

| RONNY: | Emmy, wait! |

He races after her.

MIKE comes running in from the other direction. Followed by LIZZY, JESS and TOM.

MIKE:	Has he gone?
LIZZY:	There were no police you knob head.
MIKE:	What?!?
JESS:	It was just fucking Ronny.

MIKE pisses himself laughing. He points at TOM.

MIKE:	You should have seen your face.
TOM:	I thought we were gonna get kicked out.
MIKE:	Where's the beers?
JESS:	They're finished.
MIKE:	Oh fuck. Are you serious?
JESS:	Well you are the arse who drank them all.
MIKE:	I got no money. Jess. Let's raid your place. Your mum's got heaps.
JESS:	Can you even hear what you're saying?
MIKE:	C'mon! Tonight can't finish yet. It's not fucking over yet!

MIKE remembers all of a sudden.

MIKE:	TRUTH OR DARE!
JESS:	Ugghhh. No. Fucking hell!
LIZZY:	Hey, I've still gotta do my trick.
MIKE:	No. Shut up. Truth or dare. Do me.
TOM:	Mike…
LIZZY:	Why won't you let me do my trick?

MIKE:	I didn't get my turn before. And I've got a good one. Go.
TOM:	Okay, fine. Truth or dare?
MIKE:	Truth. Ask me if I'm happy.
TOM:	That's stupid.
MIKE:	Do it!
TOM:	Fine. Are you happy?
MIKE:	No. Now ask me why not.
TOM:	Mike? Why are you doing this?
MIKE:	Ask me. Ask me.

EMILIA comes barrelling in, screaming at JESS.

EMILIA:	How could you?

RONNY follows behind.

MIKE:	Wait your turn.
EMILIA:	I could hit you. I could tear your fucking face off.
MIKE:	What…?
EMILIA:	Tell him. Tell him what happened.
JESS:	Em…
EMILIA:	How could you do this?
JESS:	What did Ronny say?
EMILIA:	You did this to hurt me.
JESS:	I didn't know.
EMILIA:	Yes you did.
MIKE:	Tell me what?
EMILIA:	You knew this would kill me.
MIKE:	Can someone tell me what the fuck is going on here?

Beat.

TOM:	Let's go for a walk.

MIKE: No. Someone tell me what's happening?

EMILIA: Tell him.

TOM: Let's go for a walk.

JESS: I kissed Tom. Ronny saw us.

Silence.

MIKE can't quite comprehend what he's hearing.

MIKE: Ah, is the important bit that you kissed him, or that Ronny saw you?

Pause.

TOM: I love her.

EMILIA buries her face in her hands. She's almost screaming into them. She can't bear it.

MIKE: You what …? Sorry? What?

He turns to JESS.

MIKE: And this just happened…?

JESS: It just happened.

MIKE: And you let it?

JESS: No. I kissed him.

MIKE: And you were planning on telling me when?

JESS: I don't know.

MIKE: You don't know?!? You were just going to not say a fucking thing 'cause why tell your boyfriend something like that?

JESS: I'm sorry Mike. I didn't mean for this to happen. But it did.

MIKE: Well, obviously.

JESS: And I don't regret it either.

It's like a knife goes through both EMILIA and MIKE.

MIKE: What did you just say?

JESS starts to cry, but stays strong.

JESS: I don't know what's happening alright? I don't even know how I feel. I'm sorry this is happening to you. But I'm not sorry that it's happened.

MIKE: I can't… I can't fucking believe this.

He turns to TOM.

MIKE: How long has this been going on? How long have you…?

TOM: Mike, don't…

MIKE: How long?

TOM doesn't say.

MIKE: I can't…

TOM: I'm sorry man.

LIZZY: Mike…

MIKE: No. I don't want to fucking speak to any of you…

He runs off.

LIZZY slowly heads off after MIKE, following at a distance.

LIZZY: Mike… MIKE…

TOM: Thanks Ronny.

RONNY: I'm sorry Tom.

TOM: I was trying to fucking tell him myself.

EMILIA is in tears. Her face buried in her hands.

RONNY goes to put his arm around her.

EMILIA: Don't touch me!

She turns to JESS.

JESS: Em… I didn't know how you felt…

EMILIA: And would it have made any difference if you did?

JESS: Yeah. It might have.

EMILIA:	It might have? Are you fucking joking?
JESS:	Well how would I know? 'Cause you never fucking said anything to me in the first place!
EMILIA:	So it's my fault is it?
JESS:	I didn't say that.
EMILIA:	You're a fucking bitch. Everything is always so easy for you isn't it?
JESS:	Are you serious?
EMILIA:	I'm sick of that one. I'll have the other one instead.
JESS:	You know that's not true. Don't you even fucking say that to me okay.
EMILIA:	Or you'll what? You'll not be my friend anymore?
JESS:	I thought we knew each other. I thought we told each other everything. Cause I've never hidden a fucking thing from you.
EMILIA:	What, like before when you let me sit there and tell you everything?

She looks to TOM.

EMILIA:	It's taken me years to tell you how I feel about him. Years.

TOM is stunned.

EMILIA:	Yeah. Surprise! Now you know.
JESS:	Em, I… Why didn't you tell me before? I didn't know.
EMILIA:	Of course you didn't. What fucking hope do I have if even you couldn't tell?

RONNY tries to put his hands on her shoulders, to calm her.

EMILIA:	Don't you dare. Don't you fucking dare. None of you even know how much this hurts.

TOM: Em…

EMILIA: Don't come near me.

She puts her hand to her nose all of a sudden.

EMILIA: Ah… not now!

She grabs a tissue from her pocket and holds it up to her nose, which starts to bleed.

TOM: Just put your head back.

EMILIA: I know how to deal with a nose bleed!

TOM reaches out to help her.

TOM: Em.

EMILIA: Don't touch me!

She turns and runs off, tears streaming down her face and a bloodied tissue pressed against her nose.

RONNY doesn't know what to do. He lets her go first but then follows behind.

JESS and TOM are left alone together.

They look at each other and both leave.

The park in silence for a moment.

MIKE walks in alone. An empty bottle gripped in his hand. He's trying to hold himself together.

A few moments later TOM enters.

MIKE: You're a fucking snake. Did you know that?

TOM: Yes.

MIKE: Ah so that's it, is it? Play the surrender card? Wear me down with your lack of spine?

TOM: No.

MIKE: Well, why are you here? What else do you want from me?

Beat.

TOM: I didn't do it to hurt you.

MIKE: So it was an accident was it?

TOM: Well it's not like you two were happy anyway.

MIKE: So you thought 'I know who can make her happier?'

TOM: I hate myself for what's going on.

MIKE: Oh I know all about your hating yourself. Don't worry about that.

TOM: Then you know I'm not doing this because I want to hurt you.

MIKE: No, you're doing it for yourself. Congratulations. You're being a selfish prick for the first time in your life.

TOM: I didn't plan this tonight. It just happened.

MIKE: Really?

TOM: It's true.

MIKE: What was it… ? 'If there's something you need to do, you should just do it. No matter what.' That's what you wrote wasn't it?

TOM says nothing.

MIKE: You didn't plan this tonight? It's been in your brain for ages.

TOM says nothing.

MIKE: You've always been a spineless shit Tom. Tonight is the first time you're not, and you can't even stand by that. You're fucking pathetic.

TOM: And you've got everything!

MIKE: Ahhh, here we go.

TOM: Have I ever done anything like this before? Tell me, have I?

MIKE: No.

TOM:	Have I even told you that I was even interested in someone?
MIKE:	It's not like you ever had a chance with anyone anyway.
TOM:	You're an arsehole. I'm not confident like you. I'm not good looking like you. I'm nothing.
MIKE:	That sounds about right.
TOM:	You think you're so good. But I'll never be like that. Do you know why? Because I can't. I'm not a selfish prick.
MIKE:	Right. Now we're getting there.
TOM:	… I don't know why I even bother.
MIKE:	Because you want me to say everything's alright. And I'm not going to.

Pause.

| MIKE: | You're trying to be me. You shouldn't. It doesn't fit. |

TOM seethes at this.

TOM:	If there is one thing I don't want to be, it's you.
MIKE:	Bullshit. You always have. Why else have you been friends with me? Because we sure as hell aren't equals.
TOM:	Shut up.
MIKE:	I don't know what I get out of it though, 'cause I wouldn't want to be like you.
TOM:	I said shut up.
MIKE:	Or what?

Beat.

MIKE:	Or what? You'll hit me?
TOM:	Don't.
MIKE:	I can do whatever I want.

Beat.

MIKE: Come on. You want to hit me?

MIKE grabs him by the collar.

MIKE: Hit me.

TOM: … Don't.

LIZZY wanders in and stands at a distance, out of their sight.

MIKE: Come on! I want you to.

TOM: STOP IT!

MIKE: HIT ME! HIT ME! DO IT! HIT ME!

MIKE suddenly kisses him.

The kiss hovers for a moment then TOM pushes him away.

He looks at MIKE for sometime, not knowing what to say.

He leaves.

MIKE knows LIZZY is there.

They both stand there in silence.

MIKE: Are you happy now?

Pause.

LIZZY walks over to him slowly.

She reaches out, slowly takes his hand.

She hugs him.

He steps away and walks off.

After a moment she follows.

RONNY comes in, calling out to EMILIA.

RONNY: EMMY? ARE YOU OKAY? HOW'S
                YOUR NOSE?

He doesn't get a response, so he sits and waits.

EMILIA walks in slowly from the toilet block.

She's carrying a bag under her arm.

It's RONNY's.

RONNY:	Hey. Are you okay?
EMILIA:	Not really. My nose is fine, but otherwise not really.
RONNY:	I'm sorry… I'm sorry for the way it all came out. I never wanted to hurt you.
EMILIA:	It wasn't your fault Ronny.
RONNY:	I know that. But I'm still sorry.
EMILIA:	Is this yours?

Beat.

RONNY:	No. Where'd you find it?
EMILIA:	Behind the toilets.
RONNY:	Someone must have left it there. It's nice. I don't know why anyone would leave a nice bag like that.
EMILIA:	No. Neither do I.

Beat.

RONNY:	How's the head going now? Better?
EMILIA:	I told my parents that I was staying at Jess's tonight.
RONNY:	Uh huh.
EMILIA:	And Tom and Mike did the same.
RONNY:	Lizzy better keep her mouth shut then. She's trouble you know.
EMILIA:	Ronny?

Beat.

EMILIA:	Who's place did you say you were staying at?
RONNY:	What?
EMILIA:	Who's place did you tell your parents you were staying at?

He looks at her for a moment. He can't answer.

EMILIA:	Your name's written inside the bag.
RONNY:	What?
EMILIA:	Your name. It's written inside.
RONNY:	Really? That's so weird.
EMILIA:	Stop it. Alright?

He doesn't say anything.

EMILIA:	Is everything okay?
RONNY:	Yeah. I mean, why wouldn't it be?
EMILIA:	Oh my god, you're more infuriating than all of them put together. I know you're sleeping in this park.

Pause.

RONNY:	I'm not…
EMILIA:	There's a sleeping bag in there.
RONNY:	I'm not. I'm just waiting things out… until I figure out what to do next…
EMILIA:	Oh Ronny.

RONNY's mask slips, and the desperately sad young man from the beginning starts to emerge.

| RONNY: | It's okay. It could be worse… |

Pause.

EMILIA:	How long have you been here?
RONNY:	A few days. Maybe a week or so.
EMILIA:	A week or so?

Beat.

| EMILIA: | You've been doing your exams and sleeping here at the same time…? |

RONNY nods.

| EMILIA: | Ronny…? Who else knows about this? |
| RONNY: | No one. |

EMILIA is struck hard by this.

RONNY:	I've been arriving early at school in the mornings… cleaning myself up in the bathrooms… I just had to get through the exams…

Pause.

RONNY:	I haven't been getting on with my dad for a while. He's been telling me I won't amount to much. He pretty much hates everything about me.

Pause.

RONNY:	We had a fight. I hit him. Then he hit me back… a lot… At least I managed to pack a bag.

Beat.

EMILIA:	What did your mum do?
RONNY:	Not much. It's not her fault.

Beat.

RONNY:	I'm not going back this time.
EMILIA:	It's happened before?

RONNY nods.

EMILIA:	You can stay at my place. You can't be here. You just can't.
RONNY:	I don't want you to tell anyone.
EMILIA:	But you can't stay here!
RONNY:	Em, please… no one can know.

Pause.

RONNY:	We've all got our secrets.

They both fall into a silence.

RONNY:	I hate school. I have for years. I've been counting down the days in my diary. A big cross through each one I got through. And

I'd look at the blank pages ahead, and I'd think… It could be okay. Those days might still be…okay.

But the closer the end of the year got… the more things weren't looking okay…

Jess asked me earlier what I was going to do? Next year…

… I can't even think about it…

'Cause when I do…there's nothing there…

Do you know how many people signed my shirt today Em?

EMILIA shakes her head.

Three. Me and two teachers.

I hate who I am. When I was a kid I never would have imagined I'd become this person. The one nobody wants to know.

I don't want to be this person anymore Em. I can't.

She pulls him in and holds him tight.

She can't let go.

And slowly they start to dance. Swaying gently from side to side.

They do it for a while.

RONNY: Em… Are we dancing?

EMILIA: No. You know I don't dance.

They keep dancing.

RONNY: But this is pretty much like we're dancing. It's a thing. It's a dancing thing, isn't it?

EMILIA: Shut up.

RONNY: Okay.

Beat.

EMILIA: Should we go find somewhere to eat?

They keep dancing slowly.

RONNY: Okay. After this.

EMILIA: After this.

They dance for a few moments longer, then they both start to head out.

He goes to pick up his bag. She gently takes it from him.

As they go to leave JESS walks in.

She and EMILIA see each from a distance. A gulf between them.

After some time JESS breaks the silence.

JESS: Can I call you?

EMILIA gently nods. Something has changed between them now though.

As they leave JESS slowly wanders back into the playground, watching them go.

LIZZY drags on a reluctant TOM…

LIZZY: Sit.

…and then MIKE, putting them on the swings.

LIZZY: Right. I don't care what anyone's got to say about it. But I'm doing my trick now whether you like it or not. Alright?

Neither of them answer.

LIZZY: Great. I can't wait to see what amazing thing you'll do Lizzy. Yay Lizzy. Woohoo!

LIZZY does her amazing trick.

LIZZY: Did you like that? I can do it naked too.

Eventually she breaks the ice and makes them smile.

LIZZY: Now talk. Properly.

She goes and sits with JESS at the back of the playground.

They all sit in silence for a while. No one willing to speak.

Eventually MIKE breaks the silence.

MIKE: Do you remember when we met?

TOM: The first day of secondary school.

MIKE: We were 11.

                         I spent the entire day being so good, and
                         sitting up so straight and not wanting to put a
                         single foot out of line. I was ready to burst by
                         the time the bell rang at the end of the day. I
                         came down here and I ran in circles. Me and
                         Oliver Maltby and Jenny Smithson. We were
                         flying around this playground. And you were
                         over there. On that slide.

                         And I was running past that tree over there
                         remember.

TOM: Yeah.

MIKE: And I went head first into the low branch.
                         Split my head wide open.

                         And I couldn't see anything because of the
                         blood, and I started calling out 'I'm blind.
                         I'm blind.'

TOM smiles at the memory.

MIKE: And then you put your hand on my shoulder
                         and said. 'My name's Tom. Do you want me
                         to go get your mum?' I said my house was
                         just around the corner and that maybe could
                         you help me home cause I didn't know if
                         I'll ever see again. So you led me back to
                         my place, where my mum screamed. 'Oh
                         my god Michael! Your face!' And when we
                         wiped the blood away you could see a big
                         chunk of tree still stuck in my forehead.

TOM: It was almost as big as your finger.

MIKE: She yanked it out and poured Dettol on it
                         and it went into my eyes and I screamed…
                         But you didn't go home.

Pause.

We played for the rest of the afternoon. You made me forget that I'd even hurt myself.

Beat.

TOM: That feels like a long time ago.

MIKE: Feels like yesterday to me.

Pause.

MIKE: How did everything go so quick?

TOM: It just did.

MIKE: But how? How did we get like this Tom. One minute we're 11, the next…

Beat.

I'm not ready. I'm not ready to say goodbye to what I was yet. I'm not ready to say goodbye to you.

TOM doesn't say anything.

MIKE: I love you Tom.

TOM: Mike…

MIKE: You're generous, and kind and you're about as different from me as humanly possible. And that's never mattered to you. You made your mind up that day you saw me with the tree sticking out of my head, that I was your friend and that was it. Am I right?

TOM nods.

MIKE: And that is something I'll never forget. For as long as I live.

They all sit quietly for a moment.

TOM: Can we still see the sun come up together?

MIKE: No.

TOM: Really…? That's a shame.

MIKE: Yeah. It is. A real shame.

Pause.

TOM: I'm sorry for what's happened.

MIKE: Yeah well, what are you going to do? My heart's broken.

Beat.

MIKE: I'm probably not going to talk to you again.

TOM doesn't say anything.

MIKE: You do understand why don't you?

TOM nods.

MIKE: Let's not make this longer than it has to be.

MIKE gets up.

MIKE: C'mon. Let's go.

LIZZY: Oh thank god. You've all exhausted me.

MIKE: Good luck in Bristol.

TOM: … Don't leave like this.

MIKE: How should we do it then?

Pause.

MIKE: So…

MIKE turns and starts to leave but stops when he sees JESS.

They don't know what to say to each other.

JESS: I love you. You know that?

MIKE nods.

She hugs him.

He leaves.

LIZZY looks at JESS and TOM.

LIZZY: He says all that now, but next week… ?

TOM: Bye Lizzy.

She hugs TOM.

MIKE calls from off.

MIKE:	LIZZY.
LIZZY:	ALRIGHT. Jess? You're amazing. I want to be like you when I'm older. Go to Mexico. Snog everyone. See you next week?

JESS smiles and nods.

LIZZY leaves.

JESS and TOM stand across from each other.

They stand there in silence for quite some time.

TOM:	What do we do now?
JESS:	I don't know.

Pause.

TOM:	What's the time?
JESS:	Just before 5.

Pause.

They head to the swings.

TOM:	What about this week. What are you doing this week?
JESS:	Ummm, I'm not sure. I guess I'll just be hanging at home. I'll have shit to deal with but at least I'll get a lie in.
TOM:	A lie in. I didn't even think of that.
JESS:	Yeah. I can't wait.

Pause.

JESS:	You're leaving on Monday?
TOM:	Yeah.
JESS:	Uh huh.

Pause.

TOM:	Hey… Happy birthday.
JESS:	… That's right. I'm an adult now.

They both share a smile.

Have you got anything planned for the next two days?

TOM: No. Not much. Just packing.

Silence.

They hold hands.

They start to swing.

They both look ahead.

The sun slowly starts to come up.

Neither of them knows what to say.

JESS: Here it comes.

They swing higher and higher.

Watching the sunrise.

THE END.